Table of Contents

This is a picture of a battle. You can see soldiers and horses falling. One man is throwing a spear. Another is just about to fall off his horse. He is holding a sword. There are dead bodies lying on the ground and a riderless horse galloping away in terror. Notice the head that has been cut off with a sword.

*The four Latin words on the picture tell us who fought in the **Battle of Hastings**. The first word means "English." In those days the English were often called **Angles**. The second word "et" means "and." The third word means "French." The people who lived in France were called "Franks." The last word, "Inprelio," means "fight." So the writing says "The English and the French fight."*

Is this how soldiers fight today? Do you think that this battle took place a short time ago? Or, did it take place a long, long time ago?

This battle happened more than 900 years ago, on 14 October in the year 1066. It was fought at a place called Hastings in southern England. It is a very famous battle.

The leader of the English soldiers was King Harold. The French forces were led by William, Duke of Normandy. Normandy is in northern France. People who lived there were sometimes called **Normans**.

We are going to find out more about this battle at Hastings in 1066 between the English and the French.

How can we really find out what happened at a battle that happened so long ago? We can look for clues in what the people in the past drew and wrote. We call this **evidence**. We are going to look at some pictures of the battle that were made soon after it ended. These clues are called **pictorial evidence**. The pictures in this chapter are examples of pictorial evidence.

The tapestry showing the Battle of Hastings is called the **Bayeux Tapestry**. For many years it hung in the cathedral in Bayeux in Normandy. The tapestry provides many pictorial clues about how people lived at the time.

Look at another picture from the tapestry. This one shows the Normans getting ready to attack England. They are carrying supplies to the boats that will sail across the English Channel.

Looking for Clues about the Past

What are the Normans carrying? You can see suits of **chain mail armour**. These suits are made of thousands of tiny metal rings fastened together. Soldiers wore chain mail armour over padded undergarments for protection when they were fighting. Notice how heavy the armour must have been. It took two people to carry one suit. Helmets are also being loaded on the boats.

In the picture the Normans are carrying weapons. We can see swords, spears, and even a battle-axe. Armies also need food and drink. One person has a barrel on his shoulder. Another is loaded down with a sack. In front is a cart loaded with weapons and a barrel of wine.

*Soon after the Battle of Hastings the Normans planned a **tapestry**. Tapestries were made to hang around the walls of drafty castles and other buildings. They kept the cold air out. This tapestry was a long roll of cloth covered with scenes or pictures of the battle. It would remind the Normans of the exciting events in their fight with the English. The pictures were stitched in coloured thread. The embroidering took two or three years to complete.*

SOMETHING TO DO

1. Make a list of the supplies that the Normans took with them to fight the battle in England.

2. The Bayeux Tapestry measures 73 m long and almost 48 cm high. Find out if your classroom is big enough to hang the Bayeux Tapestry around its walls. If not, find out if your school gymnasium is large enough. Are the walls of your school long enough?

3. Look carefully at a piece of embroidery. Notice how the stitches make a picture. Draw a simple picture about the battle on a piece of cloth. Then, stitch over the lines with coloured wool.

To find out more about the Battle of Hastings, look at three more pictures from the Bayeux Tapestry. This pictorial evidence provides us with clues.

The Normans cross the English Channel.

Route to England taken by William in 1066.

In this first picture, Duke William and his Norman soldiers are crossing the sea to England. Notice the horses on board the ships. The Normans sailed in long open boats with one mast and a square sail. The boats were steered by a large oar on the right side. When there was no wind for the sails, the boats could be rowed with smaller oars. These oars were placed along the sides of the boat.

The second picture gives us pictorial evidence of the battle itself. Here the Normans are attacking the English. All the Norman soldiers are on horseback, wearing chain mail armour and helmets. They are carrying long spears and shields. The English soldiers are in the same kind of armour. They are fighting on foot. The English are standing close together so their shields can protect them. This is called a **shield wall**.

Behind the shield wall you can see an archer firing an arrow.

Can you see that the English have arrows stuck in their shields? This means the Normans also fought with bows and arrows. The English fought back by throwing spears and axes.

At this point in the battle, the Normans on horseback have surrounded the English. It looks as if the English are going to lose the battle.

The third picture shows the death of the English king. Harold fought bravely with his soldiers. A Norman knight on horseback struck down the king with a mighty sword. By the end of the day, the English were fleeing. They had lost the Battle of Hastings.

Another way that we know about the battle is from a description written by someone who lived at that time. This clue is called **written evidence**. Look beside the last picture. There is a description of the battle by a Norman who saw it happen.

The Battle of Hastings

The Normans attack the English.

> As evening drew on, the English soldiers realized they could no longer resist. They knew that their king was dead, and his brothers with him, and many great leaders of their country. And so they turned in flight and made off at full speed. Some were on horseback, and others were on foot.

The Latin words tell us "King Harold is killed."

SOMETHING TO DO

1. Look at the map that shows the route Duke William took to get across the English Channel to Hastings. Why didn't he sail straight across the channel? Look at the picture of his ships and read the descriptions of them for clues.

2. Figure out about how far William and his soldiers travelled to get to Hastings. Place a strip of paper just under William's route. Make a mark on your paper at the place William set sail. Make another mark where he landed in France. Now, turn the paper and, keeping the second mark on the spot in France, make a third mark where William landed in England. Now measure from the third mark to Hastings. The space between the first and the last mark is the distance William travelled. Measure this distance using the scale shown on the map.

3. Describe the two kinds of evidence that you have read about that help us find out about the past.

hen the Normans won the Battle of Hastings, William became the King of England. Now King William owned most of the land in England. He needed help to keep the country under control. The king decided to keep some of the land for himself. The rest he divided among the friends who helped him conquer England. These important people were called **barons**.

In the act of homage a vassal or less powerful noble gave his loyalty to a more powerful person. Here a baron gives homage to a king.

The barons were useful to the king because they had their own armies. The king made a deal with the barons. They could have some land from the king on the condition that they would help him defend his kingdom in case of attack. They also promised to obey him and provide him with food and other supplies from the land.

At a special ceremony a noble promised to serve the king by becoming his **vassal**. The ceremony was known as the act of homage. The bare-headed vassal knelt on the ground and placed his hands between those of the king. The vassal promised to serve and help him in battle. The king accepted the pledge. In return for loyalty and service, the king gave the vassal a piece of land called a **manor**.

The barons also needed help to keep their promise and to defend the land the king had given them. They needed trained soldiers called **knights** to serve in their armies. The barons kept some of the land for themselves, and the rest they gave to the knights. In return, the knights became vassals of the barons. Knights promised to be loyal to the barons and fight in their armies.

The king, barons, and knights spent a lot of their time fighting over land. In those days, someone stronger was always trying to take their land away. They had to be ready at all times to defend their land from attack.

The king or queen and the barons spent most of their time ruling the country. The knights spent most of their time preparing to fight. None of these people had time to grow their own food. Nor did they have the special skills needed to make or sell things. These jobs were done by another class of people. The people who grew food for everyone were called **peasants** or **serfs**. The baron allowed the serfs to use small pieces of his land to grow food for themselves. In return, they had to farm the baron's land and to provide food for his family. The serfs were at the very bottom of the feudal system. They had few rights and no vassals.

Some peasants were skilled craftspeople such as bakers, blacksmiths, armour-makers, and leather workers. Others were merchants who bought and sold goods in the town markets. The barons charged the craftspeople rent and taxes for their workplaces. Merchants had to pay to put up stalls in the marketplace. The barons also took a share of all the peasants' profits.

The Feudal System

This is a diagram of the **feudal system**. In the feudal system the king or the queen was at the top. Then came the barons, and beneath them were the knights. At the bottom were the people who made up the largest social class—the serfs or peasants. Everybody except the king and queen owed service to someone higher up. They either fought or farmed for that person. In return they were given land and protection. This system was necessary during times of constant danger.

SOMETHING TO DO

In groups, discuss the following questions. Record the best answers in your notebooks.

1. Why is the diagram of the feudal system shaped like a pyramid? Why are so few people at the top and so many at the bottom? Do you think a serf could ever become a knight or baron?

2. What service could people provide for those who protected them? Which is more difficult to provide—food or safety? Why?

3. Which level on the feudal pyramid had the most power? Which level had the least power? Why?

4. How did land ownership become tied to military service?

 here is another way we can find out about the past. We can look for clues left behind in objects, big and small. We call this **physical evidence**. Castles are examples of physical evidence. A castle was a fort. Only rich and powerful people owned castles in the Middle Ages.

A motte and bailey castle.

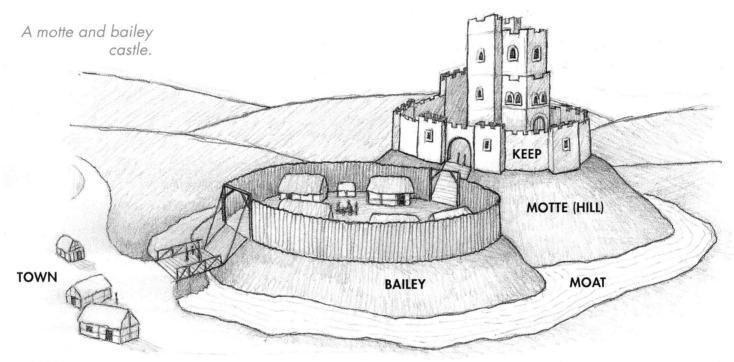

TOWN

KEEP

MOTTE (HILL)

BAILEY

MOAT

Look at this section of the Bayeux Tapestry. Five men with picks and shovels are building a hill or mound. The safest place for a castle to be built was at the top of a hill. If there was no hill, one would have to be built. The Normans called these **mottes**.

NORMAN CASTLES

One of the first things the Normans did in England was to build castles in every important town where the lord and the lady could be safe from attacks. The first castles built by the Normans were made of wood. Later they built castles made of stone. These were much stronger than the wooden castles.

In the picture of the castle on this page, you can see the motte or hill clearly. You can also see a large ditch or **moat** around it. On the motte is a stone building called the **keep**. The walls of the keep are 3.5 metres thick. The keep has three floors and a huge cellar underground. The lord, his family, and the lord's soldiers lived in the keep.

Notice that beside the motte is an earth mound surrounded by a wall and a moat. It is called a **bailey**, which means "a safe area." The lord of the castle could keep his animals and food supplies there safely. In the bailey there are barns, stables, kitchens, and workshops.

There is a narrow passageway from the bailey to the motte. The keep of a castle has double protection. First, attackers would have to get into the bailey. Then they would have to fight their way through the narrow passage before they could attack the castle keep. This type of early Norman castle was called a **motte and bailey**.

CONCENTRIC CASTLES

As time went on, castles became stronger and even more difficult to attack. They had two or more rings of defence. The castles were planned as a series of smaller and stronger rings, one inside the other. This type of castle was called **concentric**. Thousands of concentric castles were built all over Europe.

Here is a view of a concentric castle. The space in the centre of the castle is known as the **inner ward**. In the inner ward you find the castle keep and an open space where children could play and soldiers could train. The inner ward is closed in by a very high wall called the **inner curtain**. This wall could be five metres thick and thirteen metres high. The area outside this high wall is called the **outer ward**. The outer ward holds workshops and stables, vegetable gardens and animals.

At the edge of the outer ward is another wall called the **outer curtain**. The outer curtain is lower than the inner curtain. This means soldiers on inside walls could fire over the heads of the defenders on the outside walls.

Around the entire castle is a moat filled with water. The moat made it much more difficult for the enemy to get to, and climb over, the outer curtain.

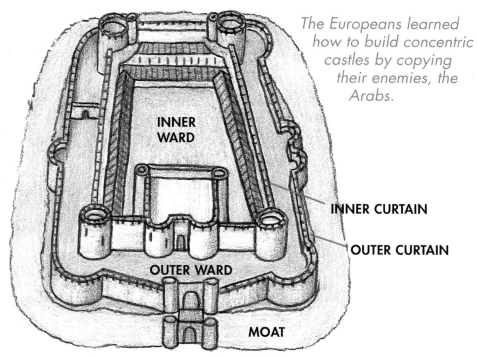

INNER WARD

INNER CURTAIN

OUTER CURTAIN

OUTER WARD

MOAT

The Europeans learned how to build concentric castles by copying their enemies, the Arabs.

Tall round towers are located along both the inner and outer curtains. Soldiers in the towers could watch in all directions for approaching enemies.

When the castle builders cut a door through the wall they had to make sure the opening was protected from attack. They strengthened the gate by building massive U-shaped towers to defend it. This part of the castle is called the **gatehouse**. It is protected by heavy wooden doors and a bridge over the moat. The bridge could be raised during an attack.

Today, many castles that you can visit or see in pictures are in ruins. This means that you have to be a detective and look for clues that tell you what the castle was like when people lived in it.

DID YOU KNOW?

Building one castle in England in the 1290s required 400 stonemasons, 30 blacksmiths and carpenters, 400 carriers, and 2000 labourers.

SOMETHING TO DO

1. Which would be harder to capture, the motte and bailey castle or the concentric castle? Give reasons for your choice.

2. Physical evidence gives clues about the past. Castles are one example of physical evidence. Brainstorm a list of other examples of physical evidence that might tell us about life in the Middle Ages.

The keep is where the lord of the castle lives with his family, knights, servants, and friends. It is a draughty and cold place to live. The only heat comes from large, open fireplaces. There are very few windows. The grey stone walls make it a dark and gloomy place. Look at the cutaway drawing of a castle keep. It will give you some idea of what it was like to live in a keep.

*The main staircase is in the tower near the entrance. It is the only way to get from one floor to the next. This is a **spiral staircase**. The steps go around a central pillar which is on the right as you go up. The staircase is built this way for protection. Imagine an enemy trying to capture the tower. It would be hard to use a sword while climbing the stairs. The central pillar on the right would always be in the way. Someone defending the tower from above would have lots of room to swing his sword.*

The main entrance to the keep is at the top of a steep flight of steps. Notice that you have to turn on the top step to go through the door. This makes it much harder for enemies to use a battering ram to knock down the door.

*Next to the storage room in the cellar is a large kitchen. It contains ovens for baking bread and fireplaces for cooking and smoking meat. Water for washing is piped into the kitchen from a stone tank on the roof called a **cistern**.*

Inside a Castle Keep

This is the bedroom of the lord's family. They sleep in **canopied beds** to keep warm. A canopied bed has a top over it and is surrounded by thick curtains on all sides to keep out draughts. Herbs such as lavender are spread on the straw mattresses. Their strong scent makes the bed smell sweeter and keeps away fleas. Several of the lord's servants sleep in the same room. His dogs and children also sleep here.

Each castle has its own chapel. Worship services are held in the chapel for the people who live in the castle.

The lord and his family live mainly in this area called a **Great Hall**. Meals are served at long tables. The lord is surrounded by friends. He receives messengers and important guests in this hall. The social life of the castle is centred here. Knights eat in the Great Hall and most of them sleep here.

The basement has a deep **well**. The well is vital to the castle. It supplies the drinking water for everyone living in the keep. The basement is also used for storage. Supplies of bacon, salt pork, cheese, flour, sugar, spices, wild game, and wine are kept here. A separate room is used as a prison when necessary.

SOMETHING TO DO

1. The picture shows you the inside of a castle keep. What clues are there to tell you about the ways the castle was used?

2. Why was it important to have supplies of food and water stored in the keep?

3. Here is a riddle. The spiral staircase would not be a problem for all attackers. Which enemy soldiers would be able to use their swords easily and still climb the stairs? Why?

easts were held at the Great Hall. Imagine you have been invited to attend a feast to honour the visit of the king. Candles glow on the tables. A covering of fresh straw has been spread on the floor. The straw makes the stone floor seem warmer. It also helps to soak up any spills from the table.

Tonight's Menu

Boar's Head with Spice Sauce
Chicken, Pheasants, and Wild Birds
Stuffed Suckling Pig
Venison boiled in Milk and Wheat
Carrots, Turnips, and Parsnips
Pine Nuts in Honey and Ginger
Date and Prune Custard
Apples and Figs
Fruit Tarts
Wine

The king sits in a place of honour with the lord and lady of the castle and the other important guests. They are seated behind a long table on a raised platform at one end of the Hall. They can look down on all the guests. This is called the **high table**. The rest of the guests sit on benches at long tables around the walls of the room.

You notice that there are no forks on the table. There are knives and spoons, however. You are going to have to eat with your fingers. Sometimes only the guests at the high table use plates. The rest of the people are given thick slices of dark, stale bread to put their food on. After the feast, this bread is given to feed the poor.

A small army of servants carry in trays of food from the kitchen. Rich people can afford to eat a wide range of food. There are different kinds of cooked meat and fish. Tonight there are elaborately roasted swans or pheasants stuffed back into their skins. There are many sweet and

spicy dishes as well. The king is served first, but only after a sample of the food has been tasted by a servant. This is to make sure that the food is not poisoned. Then the other diners are served.

With your knife you cut off a chunk of meat or fish. When the meat has been cleaned from the bones, the bones are thrown on the floor for the dogs to fight over. People eat most of the meal with their fingers and then wipe them on the tablecloth.

Travelling musicians called **minstrels** entertain the guests with music. They also tell the news about life in the world outside the castle. After the feast, a group of acrobats puts on a display of tumbling. They juggle apples, catch knives, perform tricks, and jump through hoops. The minstrels also entertain with trained bears, dogs, and monkeys who dance. Everyone at the feast cheers loudly for the music, games, and stories.

Minstrels play musical instruments and sing ballads about love and the brave deeds of knights.

SOMETHING TO DO

1. Plan the entertainment for a feast. Divide into four or five groups. Each groups decides what they will do to entertain the guests at a feast. You might put on a play together, or you might plan to do something that is mentioned in the text. Have a feast and let each group perform before the class.

2. The minstrels carried news about people and events from village to village. How do we learn about these things today?

 hen an army of knights tried to capture a castle, it was called a **siege**. There were two ways to lay siege to a castle. The attackers could surround a castle and then wait for the people inside to run out of food and water. This could take a very long time, especially if the people inside had a large supply.

A faster way to besiege a castle was to try to get inside the walls. The picture on pages 16 and 17 shows this kind of siege.

Those defending a castle had the protection of high, thick castle walls. When a castle was attacked, the defenders first sent down showers of arrows. The castle walls had narrow openings called arrow slits. Soldiers could safely fire arrows through these slits at the attackers. The **arrow storm** could be so fierce that the attackers had to shelter under their wooden shields. Heavy stones and fire were also dropped from the castle walls. Following are some of the machines used to attack a castle.

Mining under the walls was another method of attack. First, a tunnel was made under the wall. The roof of the tunnel was held up by wooden beams. When the tunnel was finished, the attackers set fire to the beams. The roof would collapse and stones from the wall would fall down into the tunnel. This left an opening into the castle at the bottom of the wall.

A **flaming catapult** was a machine used to set besieged castles on fire. It worked much like a mangon. The arm was drawn back. When the pressure was released, the arm came forward and hit a ball of flaming tar. The tar would land inside the castle walls, setting buildings and supplies on fire.

A **battering ram** was a machine used to break through walls. Attackers would first fill in part of the moat with logs and earth. Then they built a shed at the foot of the wall. The roof of the shed protected them from attack from above. Inside the shed, a thick tree trunk was hung by chains. One end of the trunk was sharpened and covered with iron. This pointed end was aimed at the wall. Soldiers swung the battering ram back and forth until it broke through the wall.

A **mangon** was a machine that could hurl heavy rocks at the castle wall. It had an arm which was drawn back under great pressure. When the pressure was released, the arm would shoot forward, firing a missile.

A Castle under Attack

A heavy timber grill called a **portcullis** could be lowered to block the entrance to the castle. The portcullis was built to slide up and down in grooves cut into the walls. The bottom end of each timber was sharpened and covered with iron. If the attackers broke through the portcullis, they still had to get through heavy wooden doors.

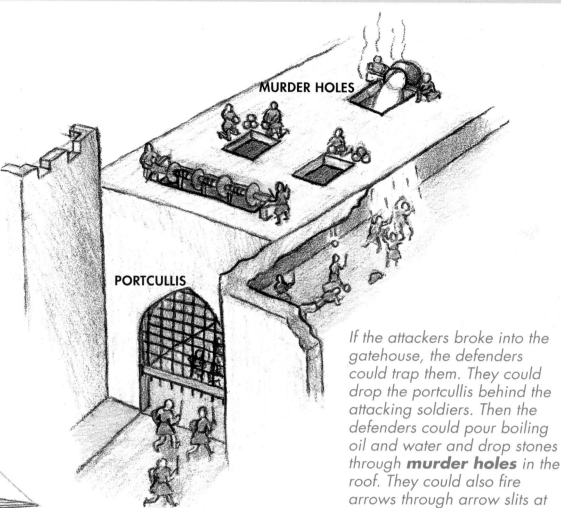

MURDER HOLES

PORTCULLIS

If the attackers broke into the gatehouse, the defenders could trap them. They could drop the portcullis behind the attacking soldiers. Then the defenders could pour boiling oil and water and drop stones through **murder holes** in the roof. They could also fire arrows through arrow slits at the sides.

A **siege tower** was a high tower on wheels used to gain entry into the castle. It could be rolled alongside the wall. The attackers would climb up inside the siege tower. At the top, they lowered a drawbridge and tried to cross over onto the top of the castle wall. The outside of the tower was covered with animal skins. This protected the soldiers inside from arrows that were fired at them from the castle.

SOMETHING TO DO

1. Pretend you are a newspaper reporter. Write an eyewitness account of the siege shown on pages 16–17. Decide whether or not the attackers succeed. Tell how they get into the castle or how the defenders keep them out.

2. Make an organizer with four columns. In the first column, name each of the weapons you see in the picture. In the second column, place a check mark if this weapon was used to lay siege to the castle. In the third column, place a check if this weapon was used to defend the castle. In the fourth column, describe how this weapon worked.

nights who rode out to battle wore suits of armour to keep them safe. You have probably seen pictures of knights dressed in shining metal armour from head to toe. Such a suit is only one kind of armour. Armour does not have to be made of metal. **Armour** is protective covering of any kind.

A knight's armour about 1100.

Some animals are born wearing armour. For example, a turtle has a shell and a rhinoceros has thick-folded skin for protection. People do not have this kind of natural armour. They have to make their own.

Knights who fought at the Battle of Hastings wore chain mail armour and helmets with nosepieces. Chain mail was made of thousands of tiny metal rings linked together. This kind of armour protected most of the body from arrows, but was not much use against spears or battleaxes. Each ring was linked to four others and held together by a tiny rivet.

In the years after the Battle of Hastings, weapons became more deadly. Soldiers needed stronger protection. By the 1400s, knights rode into battle wearing complete suits made of metal plates. The knight had to be measured. Then the armour was cut from sheets of metal and a suit was made to measure. A suit of armour covered almost every part of the knight's body, including the face. The armour was designed with flexible joints to allow the knight to move.

A new set of armour usually came with a dent somewhere in it. The armour-maker tested the suit by firing an arrow at it from close range. The arrow would dent a good suit of armour, but not make a hole. This proved to the knight who was buying the armour that it would protect him in battle.

A typical suit of armour weighed 23 to 27 kg. A knight could be in grave danger if he fell off his horse during a battle. Even if he was not injured, he could not get up quickly. He could be captured easily. So the enemy always tried to aim at the knight's horse to bring it down. For this reason, some very wealthy knights had armour made for their horses!

Another disadvantage of wearing armour was the heat. Think about getting into a closed car on a hot summer day. Imagine how hot it must have been inside a suit of metal armour. The knight had to wear protective undergarments, and he had to fight as well. He must have been sweltering!

When knights rode into battle wearing full armour, their faces were hidden. They identified themselves by carrying shields showing a coat of arms. This allowed everybody to tell which side was which on the battlefield. Every baron had a banner or flag showing his own colours. Such banners were important rallying points for knights during battles.

When people started fighting with guns and bullets, suits of armour disappeared. To protect the body from bullets, armour would have to be so thick that it would be far too heavy to wear.

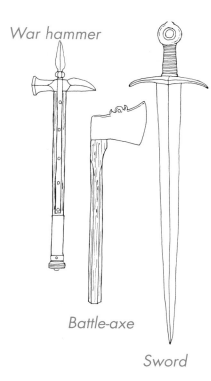

War hammer

Battle-axe

Sword

A knight's armour had to be strong enough to protect him against weapons like these.

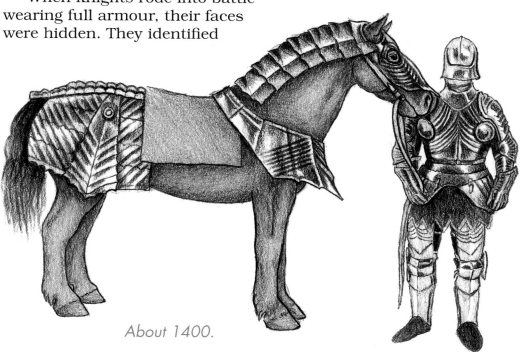

About 1400.

SOMETHING TO DO

1. Study the pictures of two types of armour. Make a list of the differences you see in the two types. How did armour change between 1100 and 1400? Why do you think it changed?

2. Artists often show knights on beautiful racehorses. Actually, their horses were more like the heavy workhorses found on farms. Tell why you think a knight needed to ride a heavy workhorse.

3. Being a knight was a job that required wearing special protective clothing. Today, a deep-sea diver wears a nylon wetsuit for protection from cold water. Name other jobs where protective clothing helps people to do their jobs more safely. For each job, describe the type of clothing worn.

4. If possible, try to plan a visit to a museum that displays the armour of the Middle Ages.

nights always had to be ready to go and fight. One way knights kept in shape between battles was to take part in **tournaments**. A tournament was a contest in which knights and horses took part in a mock battle. It was a good way to train knights and their horses for battle.

The tournament was held in a meadow outside the castle walls. The fenced-in area where the events took place was called the **lists**. The ladies and nobles watched from colourful tents on one side of the field. On the other side, the ordinary people stood to watch the events.

One popular event was called the **tourney**. Two groups of knights gathered at opposite ends of the field. When the trumpets sounded, the two armies charged. The horses thundered toward each other. The air was filled with clouds of dust. Spears clanged against shields. Lances crashed against armour. The spectators cheered for their favourites. Squires rushed forward to help their knights get back on their horses. When the dust had cleared, the army that had the most knights still on their horses won the tourney.

Another popular event at a tournament was the **joust**. This was a contest of fighting skills of individual knights. Two knights on horseback galloped headlong toward each other from opposite

ends of the field. Each tried with all his strength to knock the other to the ground with his lance. The knight who won claimed the horse and armour of his opponent.

For good luck, a knight often wore a brooch or scarf of his favourite lady. He tried to bring honour to the lady by winning the joust.

Tournaments were costly in many ways. Knights and horses were injured and sometimes killed. Lances, swords, and suits of armour were ruined. The noble who held the tournament had to feed hundreds of guests and provide the prizes. However, tournaments were popular in spite of their costs. People thought that a knight who did not fight well in a tournament would not fight well in battle.

An account written in the Middle Ages tells how the knight named Ipomydon fought in a tournament.

Plenty of great knights came there dressed for the tournament. A thousand were present armed with lance and sword. Knights began to fight. On all sides they were unhorsed. That day Ipomydon was victorious. There he ran many a course. With his lance he struck all he met, and flung both horse and rider to the ground. The judges gave him the prize—a thousand pounds.

SOMETHING TO DO

1. What was the purpose of holding tournaments? Describe the events of a tournament that helped to serve their purpose.

2. "People thought that a knight who did not fight well in a tournament would not fight well in battle". In small groups discuss the meaning of this sentence. Do you think that people were right in thinking this? Why?

3. In the evening in the Great Hall, knights told tales about their achievements in tournaments. Pretend you are Ipomydon. Write a creative story about your success.

odfrey was the young son of a rich man. When he was seven years old his parents bought him a horse. Then they sent him to the baron's castle to begin his training to become a knight.

Pages polished their knight's armour keeping it bright and shining. The pages learned how to clean rusty chain mail armour by rolling it in a barrel of sand.

The first step on the stairway to becoming a knight was that of a **page**. Godfrey and the other pages helped the knights put on their armour and horses.

Godfrey was trained to ride a horse. Every knight had to feel at home on horseback. He had to be able to control his horse with one hand so that the other hand was free to hold a lance.

When Godfrey turned fourteen, he became a **squire**. He was chosen to serve a baron named Simon. It was Godfrey's duty to look after Simon's armour and horses. At mealtime, Godfrey carried water to Simon for washing his hands. He carved Simon's meat and filled his cup when it was empty. Godfrey rode with Simon to tournaments and battles carrying his shield and weapons.

Squires had to grow strong and tough for battle. Much of

THE CODE OF CHIVALRY

Chivalry means the way of life of the knights. Chivalry required a knight to be:

- loyal to his lord
- faithful to the lady he loved
- loyal to the church
- a protector of the weak, the poor, the helpless, and all women and children
- a brave and well-trained fighter who could bear suffering and hardship
- fair, kind, just, and truthful

One popular sport was charging at a **quintain**, a dummy made to look like a knight. The quintain was hung on a pole so that it would swing around. The squire charged on horseback at the quintain. If the squire did not hit it in the right spot, the dummy would swing around and hit him.

Baron Simon makes Godfrey a knight.

their time was spent in fighting and wrestling with each other. All of their games were meant to strengthen their bodies and train them for warfare.

By the time Godfrey was seventeen, he was ready to go into battle. Godfrey fought bravely alongside Simon. He proved to be a fine and brave warrior.

No one was born a knight.

Knighthood had to be earned. One day in battle Godfrey helped to save his baron's life. Baron Simon made Godfrey a knight right on the battlefield. Godfrey knelt down and the Baron touched him lightly on the shoulder with the flat part of his sword. This act was called the ceremony of **dubbing**. Godfrey promised to be a loyal and brave knight.

SOMETHING TO DO

1. What training did a boy need to become a knight? Explain why each part of his training was necessary.

2. In 1200 a knight's warhorse was worth several hundred sheep. Without his own horse a boy could not become a knight. Why did only the sons of wealthy families become knights?

3. In groups discuss the Knight's Code of Chivalry. Then write "A Code of Chivalry" for your classroom.

here were few opportunities open to women during the Middle Ages and little chance to get an education. Peasant women had to work for a living. They toiled beside their husbands in the fields and had to feed and clothe their families.

A noblewoman bids her husband farewell as he leaves for battle. Noblewomen often helped their husbands to run their estates. If her husband was away at the king's court or on Crusade, the lady was left in charge. She settled disputes, handled the finances, and managed the farm. Some women even fought to defend their castles when they were under siege. In the Middle Ages, however, the main duty of the wife of a noble was to raise children and look after the household.

For girls from wealthy families, there were really only two choices. They either got married or became a nun. Most marriages were arranged by the parents. The bride's family gave the husband-to-be a **dowry**. This was an amount of money or possessions that the bride brought into the marriage. Most nobles looked for wives with large dowries. Child brides were not uncommon. Most girls could expect to be married by age fourteen. Those who were not married by the time they were twenty-one would probably stay single for the rest of their lives.

Some unmarried women entered nunneries or convents where they devoted their lives to serving God. In a convent, women could obtain an education and perhaps take on the responsibility of managing a large farm. Many convents were large landowners, and the nuns were important community leaders.

A noblewoman was also expected to train young girls from other castles in the duty of running a household. Noblewomen also had a role in training young pages. Ladies taught pages to sing, dance, and perhaps to play a musical instrument. They told the boys exciting stories of knights and heroes. Pages ran errands for the ladies of the castle. From the women they learned to be courteous, well-mannered, and obedient.

Some women learned skilled trades. They worked with their husbands or fathers in their workshops. Some became tradeswomen in their own right. Silk weaving in London was almost entirely done by women.

Spinning and weaving were domestic chores, done by women in the house. Wool from sheep had to be spun into yarn. They used hand-held spindles onto which the wool turned into yarn as the spindle twirled. Then the yarn was woven on a loom into cloth. Children helped by untangling raw wool.

A BARON'S DAUGHTER

Eloise is the daughter of an important baron. What is her home life like?

In the morning she wakes up and gets dressed. Servants lay out the clothes she is going to put on. After breakfast Eloise helps her mother to give the daily orders to their servants. They are told which rooms to clean, which clothes and pots to wash, and what food to cook for the family's meals. The servants are ordered to make the beds and bake the bread. Then Eloise spends the rest of the morning embroidering a tapestry and spinning wool into yarn. She also finds time to play a game of chess with her brother and father.

In the afternoon she goes hunting with her father and mother. They ride horses and hunt with hawks and hounds. At night Eloise is allowed to attend the feast in the Great Hall. After the feast, as a rich baron's daughter, she sleeps in a canopied bed with a feather, straw, or horsehair mattress.

Medieval noblewomen were expected to be skilled at playing many different games. Chess was one of the most popular board games of the time.

SOMETHING TO DO

1. Hold a class discussion to plan a mural illustrating all the tasks that women performed in the Middle Ages. Then divide into smaller groups and draw the mural.

2. Make a diary entry for a day in the life of Eloise, a baron's daughter. Use these ideas to help you:

   - getting up and dressing
   - giving orders to the servants
   - walking around the castle
   - visiting all the rooms in the castle
   - watching what the servants are doing
   - enjoying pastimes and entertainments
   - attending the feast in the Great Hall.

o you remember that the king owned all the land? He kept some of it for himself. The rest he divided up into pieces of land called **manors** for his friends the barons. The barons did exactly the same thing. They kept a lot of the best land for themselves and gave the rest to their knights. All of the work was done by the peasants or serfs allowed to live on the manor.

Look at the picture of a typical manor. Locate the lord's manor house. It is not as grand as the castle of a king or a wealthy baron. It is the smaller house of a knight. It is made of stone and is surrounded by a wall for protection. There are stables for the knight's horses and kennels for his hunting dogs. The house has a large garden where vegetables, herbs, and fruit trees grow. There are many beehives because honey was the main way of sweetening food. Sugar had to be brought from the East, so it was very expensive. The lord also had pieces of land in the big fields.

Today most farmers live on their farms. In the Middle Ages, most serfs did not live on the land they farmed. They lived in huts or cottages in the village of the manor. Locate the part of the village where the serfs lived.

In the sketch of the manor you can see three big fields where the serfs grew food. These fields were large with no fences. They were divided into long narrow strips. Some of the strips belonged to the lord of the manor. The serfs farmed this land for him. The serfs were allowed to farm a few strips for themselves. These strips were scattered all over the three fields so that everybody had some good land and some poor land.

Part of the manor was kept as common land and pasture. All the people of the village were allowed to send their animals to the common to graze. Children were sent to look after the animals.

Another part of the manor was left as wild forests. Only the lord and his guests hunted in the forest. If serfs were caught hunting there, they were punished severely.

The lord provided a mill where the serfs had their grain ground into flour. Millers were not popular people at this time. That is because the serfs were forced to use the lord's mill and pay whatever fee the miller demanded.

Nearly every village had a church. Notice that the church is a large building for a small village. What does this tell you about the importance of religion to the people of the manor?

The lord did not work in the fields. The serfs raised all the food and produced other goods needed by the lord, his family, and his friends. The manor was almost totally **self-sufficient**. This means that the work of the serfs and the manor lands produced most of the things everyone needed. Serfs grew all the grain and vegetables that were required. Animals were raised to provide meat. The serfs made

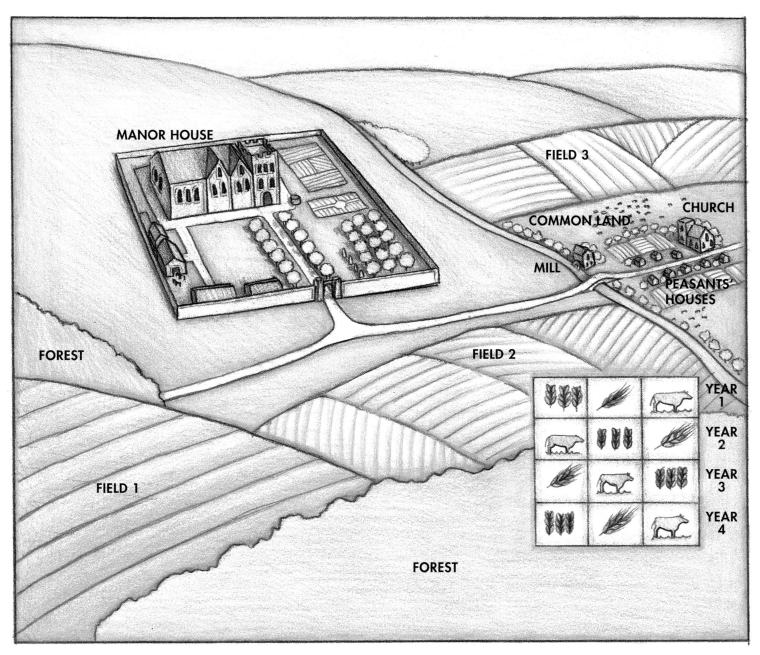

their own bread, butter, and cheese. They made their own clothes from the cloth they wove on their own looms. About the only things not produced on a manor were salt, spices, sugar, iron, silk, and fine cloth. The lords and ladies of the manor bought these goods from merchants in the towns.

In one year the first field was planted with wheat that was ground into flour. The second field was planted with barley to make beer. The third field was not planted and was allowed to rest. Cows and sheep grazed on it. Their manure helped to make the third field grow good crops next year. Every year the crops were changed.

SOMETHING TO DO

1. A serf's strips of land were scattered all over the manor fields. In one way this was an advantage. It made sure that the good and the bad land were shared equally. Think of the disadvantages of dividing the land this way.

2. List the products that could be made from things grown or raised on the manor.

et's visit the cottage of Tom and Elizabeth. They are serfs on the manor owned by Baron Robert. Elizabeth and Tom live in a tiny, low two-room cottage. It is built of planks and the walls are made of mud and straw mixed together. The roof is covered with bundles of straw tied together. It is called a **thatched roof**. The floor is dirt, packed down hard.

These pictures show the steps in building a serf's cottage. Serfs needed lots of wood. They used it to make the frames of their cottages.

The photograph shows what the finished cottage must have looked like. This cottage has a shingled roof, but when it was built it had a thatched roof.

The inside of Tom and Elizabeth's cottage is really quite dark. There is only one window. Glass is too expensive so the window is covered with an oiled animal skin. The picture on page 29 shows what the inside of the cottage probably looked like. What is the furniture like? Who built the furniture? Notice that there are no armchairs or soft springy beds. Where does the family sleep? There is no fireplace and no chimney. A fire for cooking and warmth is away from the walls in the middle of the floor. This is to avoid setting fire to the house.

Many of the best things produced by the hard work of the serfs go to the table of Baron Robert. Poor people like Tom and Elizabeth eat only two meals a day. Suppose during our visit we are invited to stay for a meal. What would we eat? For breakfast there is a chunk of dark bread, goat's cheese, and a bit of porridge. For the evening meal, oatmeal, beans, and a rabbit might be cooked together in a large pot over the fire. A stew like this was eaten with bread. Most poor people hunted wild animals or fished to add to their diet. But if they were caught **poaching** (hunting or fishing without permission) on the lord's lands, they would be severely punished.

A writer named Geoffrey Chaucer wrote a poem in which he described the cottage of a poor woman. It was written in old English. You will have to put it into modern English before you answer the questions. The meanings of the difficult words are given on page 29.

> *Three large sowes hadd she,*
> *Three kyn, and eek a sheep.*
> *Ful sooty was hir bour, and eek her halle,*
> *In which she eet full many a sclendre meel.*

Old English	Meaning
sowes	sows, female pigs
kyn	cows
eek	also
bour and halle	the two rooms in the cottage
sclendre	slender

1. How many animals did she have?
2. Why was the inside of the cottage sooty?
3. What were the two rooms in the cottage called?
4. How do you know the woman was poor?

SOMETHING TO DO

1. Make a chart like this in your notebook to compare Elizabeth and Tom's cottage with the place where you live.

	Serf's Cottage	My Place
What is the house made of?		
How many rooms are there?		
How is the house heated?		
Number of tables, chairs, beds and benches.		
What are the windows made of?		

2. How were the meals of the serfs different from the meals served in the castle?

3. Write a poem about the way the serfs lived in the Middle Ages.

The English poet Geoffrey Chaucer.

lizabeth's day starts very early. At 4:00 a.m. she gets up to build the fire. Then she starts the porridge and sets the table for breakfast. When the cottage has warmed up, Elizabeth wakes the family and dresses the children. By 6:00 a.m. she and Tom are at work in the fields.

1. What does the serf use to pull his plough?

2. What are the jobs of each of the people in the picture?

This painting from a medieval manuscript shows how farmers sowed seed in their fields. Why do you think there are so many birds in the picture?

Elizabeth's job is to walk beside the plough and drive the ox with a stick. Tom guides the plough to break up the soil. While she is working in the fields, Elizabeth tries to keep an eye on the baby and the smaller children. There are no day-care centres or babysitters. By the time they are five or six, the children will be helping their parents in the fields.

Three days each week Tom must work on Baron Robert's land. The **bailiff** is the lord's trusted servant who is in charge of getting the farm work done. The bailiff tells the serfs what work has to be done. Besides working in the fields, Tom supplies the manor house with firewood. He also helps to fill in the potholes in the road. Sometimes he looks after the sheep to protect them from wild animals.

During planting and harvesting, Tom is expected to work even longer hours for the lord. The rest of the week, Tom and Elizabeth work on their own strips of land.

After working hard in the fields all day, Elizabeth must prepare the simple evening meal. The rest of her evening is spent weaving cloth, mending clothes, or baking bread.

As you can see, serfs were almost always busy with back-breaking work. Men and women worked side by side through the cold of winter and the heat of summer. Everyone got up before sunrise and worked until dark to grow enough food for the people of the manor.

This picture shows how grain was piled onto the carts. Then it was hauled by horses to the lord's barn. There it was spread out on the floor. Serfs beat out the kernels of grain with long sticks called **flails**. The kernels of grain could be ground into flour at the lord's mill. Flour was used to make bread, which was the main food eaten by serfs.

1. Describe the instrument used to cut the grain. It is called a **scythe**.

2. What is done with the ripe grain after it is cut?

Besides farming, there were other jobs to be done in the village. A blacksmith fashioned all the metal things the villagers used. What is the blacksmith making in this picture? Think of other objects made of metal the villagers would need.

SOMETHING TO DO

1. Find out how each of the farm activities shown in the pictures is done today. Make a chart to compare how the different activities were done in the Middle Ages and how they are done today. Try to find pictures in magazines to illustrate modern farming techniques.

2. Working in groups, make a mural that shows spring, summer, and fall farm activities in the Middle Ages. Re-read the section on the Manor for details on how the land was farmed. Write a sentence at the bottom of your mural to explain your scenes.

 ou have seen how hard the serfs had to work. Even the smallest children had chores. They didn't even have weekends free the way we do today. There were only a few days every year when everybody could relax and have fun.

As this picture from a medieval manuscript shows, both men and women enjoyed hunting with hawks. When the bird was not hunting, a little leather hood was put over its head to keep it calm. As soon as the hunter spotted some prey, the hood was removed and the bird was allowed to hunt. Hawking provided fun and sport. It also put fresh meat on the table in the winter months.

On holy days such as Christmas and Easter, everyone took a holiday. May Day was Elizabeth's favourite holiday. It was celebrated on the first day of May after the long winter. May Day marked the end of winter's dreary months and the beginning of spring. People looked forward to warmer days, new crops, and more food to eat.

On holidays, and at fairs, merchants set up stalls with things to sell. They sold cheese, salt, pots and pans, tools, knives, leather goods, and cloth. There were also travelling entertainers and musicians. Typical instruments were bagpipes, flutes, trumpets, lutes, and drums.

You have read about tournaments enjoyed by the wealthy people. Another favourite sport of the rich was **hawking**, or **falconry**. Men and women learned to train wild hawks or falcons to kill small animals and other birds. Once it had killed its prey, the hawk was trained to return to its owner's wrist carrying the dead animal. The person wore a leather glove to protect the hand from the bird's strong, sharp claws.

In the Middle Ages children of wealthy families had toys. Little girls played with dolls while boys had wooden toy soldiers and horses and spinning tops. Poor children had fewer and more simple toys. As they grew older, young people learned to dance and play musical instruments. They enjoyed writing love songs and singing them to each other.

Entertainment For All

Wealthy people also enjoyed hunting with dogs. They followed a pack of hounds to find their prey. Sometimes they would hunt for hare; other times it might be for fox. Hunts became great social events and sometimes wealthy women took part.

Jugglers, acrobats, and dancing bears were popular forms of entertainment at fairs. There were games, sports, and dancing. Children loved playing blind-man's-buff and pick-a-back. Have you played these games yourself?

SOMETHING TO DO

Gather in groups to discuss the following questions.

1. How were the games and sports of the serfs different from those of the wealthy? Who had more fun? Why?

2. What games or sports could you photograph today that are similar to the ones that are shown here?

DID YOU KNOW?

Children in the Middle Ages played a version of hockey. The ball was probably made from an animal's bladder.

he Christian church played a very important part in the daily life of the village. The Catholic Church was a powerful force in the Middle Ages. There was no other Christian church at that time. There were, however, two other leading religions in Europe in the Middle Ages. They were Islam and Judaism.

A medieval church in England. Hunted criminals were safe from arrest if they took shelter in a church. Every church had the right to protect persons running from the law. This was called giving **sanctuary**. *A person who reached the church and got hold of its doorknocker was safe from capture.*

Whether they were rich or poor, most Christian men and women were married and buried by the church. People went to church every Sunday to pray and to worship. Churches were not just places of worship. They were like art galleries because they were filled with statues, carvings, and paintings of saints and Bible characters. Most glorious of all were the windows of coloured glass. These **stained glass windows** told Bible stories in pictures for those who could not read.

The church yard was an important centre in village life. People held meetings there to decide things about the crops and animals. Sometimes important business deals were made in the church porch. No one would back out of a deal made on church property. Plays, markets, and fairs were held in the church yard.

The men who ran the churches were called priests. In the village, the priest was second in importance to the lord of the manor. Often the priest was the only person in the village who could read and write. He had to be educated, since services were said in Latin. The priest also told stories from the

This stained glass window from a church shows Saint Martin cutting his cloak in half to share it with a beggar. The lesson is clear: show charity to those less fortunate than yourself.

Bible and explained the church's rules about how people should live.

Most priests were wise and kind and did lots of good things for the villagers. There was no one else to help ordinary people but the church. Priests tended the sick and tried to help the poor. They listened to people's problems and gave them advice.

Here is a story about a priest and some serfs. It comes from *Aesop's Fables*, one of the first books printed in England.

The Village Church

A priest sits alone by his fireside. Suddenly, he hears a loud knocking at his door. In come some serfs. They are very angry about the way they are being treated by the lord. They complain that the lord and his friends have been trampling on their crops while hunting, and about other things too.

At last the priest holds up his hand for silence. No doubt these wrongs must be put right, but first the serfs must listen to his story.

Once upon a time there were some rats and mice. They were troubled by a very large, mean cat who chased them and pounced upon them. One night, while the cat slept, the rats and mice held a meeting. They decided that something must be done about the cat. One rat had the clever idea of tying a bell around the cat's neck. This way they would hear him coming and be able to escape. All agreed it was a fine idea.

"But," said a mouse, "Which one of us will be brave enough to tie a bell on the cat?" While they were thinking about this problem, the cat woke up and sent them scurrying away in terror.

"So you see my friends," said the priest, "you will have to decide who will bell the cat. Which of you is brave enough to tell the lord and his hunting friends that they must change their ways?"

The serfs scratched their heads and muttered excuses. This one has some ploughing to do; that one has a sick wife to nurse; another one must look after his pigs. One by one they shuffled away. The priest is left alone again by his fireside. The priest's cat comes along and, sitting beside him, begins to wash its face with its paws.

SOMETHING TO DO

1. What complaints did the serfs have against the lord and his friends?

2. Do you think the serfs had a right to be angry? Why?

3. What are some of the ways the priest could help the serfs with their problem? What is the best solution? Why is it the best solution?

4. Why do you think the priest told the serfs this story?

5. Locate a copy of *Aesop's Fables* in your library. Read some more of Aesop's stories. Find out why they are called fables.

ome men and women devoted their whole lives to the worship of God. The men were called **monks**. The women were called **nuns**.

Monks ate simple meals of bread, cheese and vegetables.

There were no printing presses in the Middle Ages. The monks made all the Bibles and prayer books by hand. Since every word had to be copied by hand, it could take months, even years, to copy one book.

THE MONKS

When a man decided to become a monk, he had to make three main promises called **vows**. One was a vow of **obedience**. He promised to obey the head monk called the **Abbot**. Another vow was one of **poverty**. A man had to give up everything he owned. Monks did not marry. That was because they took a vow of **chastity**.

All the monks in a particular group lived in an abbey or **monastery**. Life there was very simple and very strict. Each day was divided between work and prayers. Several times a day, and even during the night, monks gathered in the church of the monastery to say prayers.

Everyone dressed alike in the monastery. The monks wore long brown, black, or white loose-fitting robes made of coarse material. A cord was tied around the waist. Sandals protected their feet. Meals were very simple. Most of the food was grown in fields just outside the abbey walls. Occasionally the monks had meat, but more often they ate fish from their ponds.

Everyone had useful work to do. Some monks did the farming. Others taught the sons of wealthy parents to read and write. Many monks were well educated and monasteries became centres of learning. In those days monks were almost the only people who wrote things down.

No monk was allowed to speak in the room where they copied the books. Only sign language was allowed. If a monk needed a reference book, he made a motion of turning pages. If he wanted a new quill pen, he held up his old one.

Books were not made of paper. They were written on **vellum** made from calfskin or **parchment** made from sheepskin. The quill pen was a goose feather, sharpened to a point and dipped in ink.

Nuns working in the kitchen made butter and cheese from the milk.

THE NUNS

Like monks, nuns made vows of poverty and chastity. They also promised to obey the head nun called the **Mother Superior**.

Nuns lived together in their own abbey called a **nunnery** or **convent**. Life there was just as simple and just as strict as it was in a monastery. The nunnery was plain and simply furnished. There was only one room, besides the kitchen, with a fire in it during the winter. Meals were eaten in silence while one nun read aloud from the Bible.

All the nuns dressed alike. They wore long black gowns and veils with white cloths tied around their faces. It did not matter that some of them had to work in the fields under the hot sun. They still had to wear these **habits.**

The nuns ran large farms. Some ploughed the fields and planted and harvested the crops. Others tended sheep and milked cows. These were sold, along with other farm products, to raise money for the abbey.

Some of this money was given as **alms** to the poor who came to the gate. Alms are donations of money or goods to the poor. The nuns also cared for sick people. This was a time when there were few hospitals. There was also no sick pay or unemployment benefits. In times of trouble, people turned to the nuns for help.

In the Middle Ages, even the daughters of wealthy parents did not always learn to read and write. But they could attend a convent school to learn proper manners and needlework from the nuns.

The pages of a book were beautifully decorated. The capital letter of the first word in a chapter was painted large in gold, crimson, or blue. Here, the first letter on the page is a "D." Inside the letter, the artist has drawn a scene from the Bible story of David and Goliath.

SOMETHING TO DO

1. Nuns and monks did not charge for their services. Their help was known as **charity**. Make a list of modern charities. How do people raise money for these charities today?

2. Choose one paragraph from this chapter to copy by hand. Work under the same conditions as the monks—no talking. Make the capital letter of the first word very large and colour it. Decorate the borders with drawings to illustrate what the paragraph talks about. Put all the paragraphs together in an illustrated book.

n abbey could be either a monastery or a convent. The one shown in the picture here was a monastery. It was like a small town. Everything, even the cemetery where dead monks were buried, was within its walls.

Monks and nuns still live in abbeys in Europe today. This is a picture of a Trappist monk in France. These monks pray seven times every day. One of these times is in the middle of the night. A passageway between the dormitory and the church makes it easy for the monks to attend night services. Dormitory comes from the Latin word "dormire," which means to sleep.

A **porter** or guard at the main gate gave directions to the various buildings. A poor visitor did not have far to go. The **alms house**, where food and money were distributed, was next to the main gate.

Those who were sick could find care in the **infirmary** or hospital. It was located in a corner of the abbey away from most of the activity. It had its own kitchen. There were two large houses at the back of the abbey. One was the **abbot's guest house**. There were very few inns or hotels in the Middle Ages, so travellers often stayed in the guest house during their journey. The larger house was the **abbot's house**. It was spacious because the abbot often entertained important guests, and sometimes even the king.

There were other buildings that were barns or storehouses. All the products from the fields were stored there.

Most of the daily activity occurred in the buildings in the centre of the picture. Four main buildings-the **church**, **scriptorium**, **dormitory**, and **refectory**-formed a square. The open space in the centre was called the **cloisters**. Some of these names come from Latin words.

To the right of the dormitory was the kitchen. All the food for the monks was prepared there. Then it was carried to the refectory or dining room. The school rooms were against the refectory wall.

The scriptorium was between the refectory and the church. Scriptorium comes from a Latin word "scribere" which means to write. Can you figure out what the monks did in the scriptorium?

The monks spent most of their leisure time in the cloisters. This open garden had covered walkways along the sides to shelter them from the weather. Often the monks strolled through these walkways with one another or sat in the cloisters to read or rest.

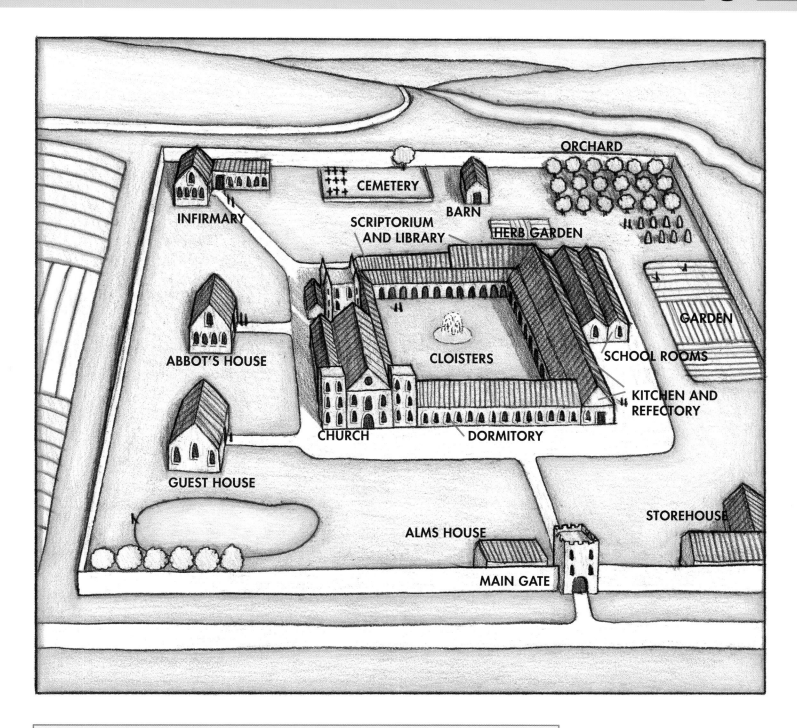

Labels on the plan: ORCHARD · CEMETERY · BARN · INFIRMARY · SCRIPTORIUM AND LIBRARY · HERB GARDEN · GARDEN · ABBOT'S HOUSE · CLOISTERS · SCHOOL ROOMS · KITCHEN AND REFECTORY · GUEST HOUSE · CHURCH · DORMITORY · ALMS HOUSE · STOREHOUSE · MAIN GATE

SOMETHING TO DO

1. Use your dictionary to find out which Latin words "refectory" and "cloisters" come from. What do these Latin words mean?

2. Work with a partner. Take turns quizzing each other. One person points to a part of the abbey. The other person must explain the purpose of that part of the abbey. Then reverse rolls.

3. In pairs or small groups, make a plan of your schoolyard like the plan of an abbey. Include things like the flagpole, playground, driveways, parking lot, drinking fountains, trees, and bushes. Is there anything about your school-yard that makes it special?

ike castles, many towns in the Middle Ages were surrounded by high walls for protection. Inside the walls, houses, shops, churches, and gardens were huddled closely together.

Notice the narrow streets in the drawing. The streets were not paved, nor were there any sewers or drains. When it rained, the townspeople had problems with puddles and mud. When it was dry, the streets were dusty and dirty. People threw their garbage into the streets to rot. Rats were everywhere.

This little town in France, called Carcassonne, still looks very much like it did in the Middle Ages. Many other medieval towns looked similar. Notice the two sets of walls and the lookout towers. Does this walled town remind you of a concentric castle?

Towns could be entered only through gateways. London, a town in England, had seven gates. Visitors could only enter by the gates when they had paid a toll. The gates were guarded by gatekeepers whose job was to open the gates at sunrise and to lock them at sunset. After nightfall, no one could enter the town without special permission.

Medieval towns were much smaller than cities today. A town of one thousand people was quite large in the 1400s. The sketches on page 41 show some of the reasons why certain towns became important centres.

Farm animals were often kept inside the walls of the town. Londoners were allowed to keep pigs in their houses, but they were not supposed to let the pigs wander in the streets. If a pig had a bell around its neck, however, that meant it belonged to the Hospital of St. Anthony. These hospital pigs were allowed to roam all over London eating the garbage in the streets. Once they grew fat, the pigs were killed to feed the patients.

Most houses were built of timber, or a timber frame with walls of plaster. Many houses had two or three floors. The upper stories hung over the streets making the streets quite gloomy and airless. These overhangs were known as **jetties**. They sometimes jutted out so far that neighbours could almost shake hands from their upstairs windows.

The townspeople walked under the overhanging parts of the buildings to avoid being hit by things thrown from the windows. Often there would be a sudden shout that sounded like, "Gardy loo." A bucket was then emptied into the street. An unfortunate passer-by could be drenched with dirty water. The cry meant, "Look out, water!" It was a careless way of saying, "Gardez l'eau."

The Growth of Towns

London was a port city on the River Thames. It became the capital of England because the king and queen lived there.

Canterbury was the home of a famous church. It became a religious centre.

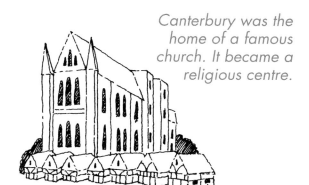

Oxford was a university town where students went to study.

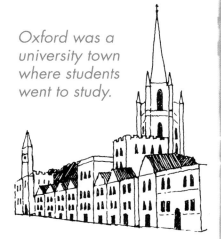

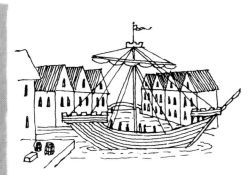

Venice was a port town on the Adriatic Sea. Many ships delivered goods there and took other goods away.

TOWN RULES

All townspeople shall put out their fires and candles when the bell rings at 9:00 p.m.

There shall be a tub full of water in front of every house at all times.

No one shall throw water from the jetty windows.

Each person shall clear the garbage from the front of the house.

No pigs shall be allowed in the town streets.

In winter months, a lantern with a lighted candle shall burn outside every house.

There shall be a ladder and a pole with a hook on the end of it in the front of every house at all times.

Paris was a town where important roads crossed. Travellers stayed there for the night.

Antwerp was a market centre where people could buy and sell goods.

SOMETHING TO DO

1. Use an atlas to locate each of the towns mentioned in this chapter.

2. In groups, brainstorm the reasons for each of the town rules. Make up a list of rules your town has to handle similar problems.

3. Make a chart to compare the pollution problems of the Middle Ages with those of today. Find or draw pictures to illustrate the problems shown in your chart. Use these to make a giant collage for your classroom.

magine we are living in a town in the Middle Ages. As we walk through the winding streets, we see tiny shops of craftspeople lining the streets. These shops are like little open booths. The workers are usually busy making the goods that are offered for sale. They and their families live behind the shop or on the floors above.

Colourful signs swing over the shop doors. They show pictures of the goods for sale—a hat for a hatmaker, basins for a barber, a unicorn for a goldsmith, and so on. Remember that very few people can read. The shopkeepers used this way to show what is sold inside.

Examine the illustration above. It shows what a shopping centre in the Middle Ages looked like in the 1400s. Tailors are busy snipping and stitching. Furriers are setting out their fur pelts. A barber is shaving a customer. Look at the basins swinging above his stall. Basins were the sign of his trade. A barber did more than cut hair and shave customers. He also pulled teeth and bled patients. **Bloodletting** was a way of treating

diseases. The barber would cut the sick person to make him or her bleed into a basin. People believed that this would get rid of the infection. In fact, many people actually got worse because of blood loss!

Look at the pastry shop on the right. Fresh pies are set out on the counter. In the Middle Ages, goods were sold directly from the maker to the user. Everything you bought you could see being made right before your eyes.

In the Middle Ages, people would **bargain** for the goods they wanted to buy. For example, a customer would ask the shoemaker the price of a certain pair of boots. The shoemaker would name a high price. The customer would offer a very low price.

Merchants and Craftspeople

If we stop for a moment and look into the shoemaker's shop, we will see young boys running errands or working with simple tools. They are **apprentices** who are learning the trade from the **master** shoemaker. The master shows the apprentices how to do their tasks. The shoemaker does some of the more difficult work. He and his workers make every part of the boots and shoes themselves.

Then the customer and the shoemaker would argue about the price. The shoemaker would mention the good points about the boots. The customer would try to find bad things. Finally, they would agree on a price between the high and low prices first mentioned. In some parts of the world, people still bargain for goods.

Songs help us to know what it was like to go shopping during the Middle Ages. Look at the verses from this song. People sang it as they opened their shops and set up their market stalls.

Here's the Dairy Woman Nell,
With her goat's milk cheese to sell;
And here's Jan who sells us fish
Eels and herring, salt or fresh.

Skilful Wat the saddler sits
Making harness, reins, and bits;
Molly brings a fine fat hen
With its chickens in a pen.

Will the Tailor makes good clothes
Jerkins, tabards, caps, and hose;
Dan the Baker kneads his dough
While his fiery ovens glow.

SOMETHING TO DO

1. Make a list of the goods that are available for sale in the song. Add to the list any other goods that are being offered for sale in the picture of the market.

2. Hold a market day. Divide into two groups, merchants and customers. The merchants bring an item to sell. The customers will be given play money. Bargain with one another for the goods. Afterwards, discuss with the class what happened.

We have already seen that there were people in the Middle Ages who **specialized** in making just one thing. People who practised the same craft often lived on the same street or in the same part of town. In London, the bakers lived on Bread Street, the tailors on Threadneedle Street, and the saddle-makers on Saddle Street.

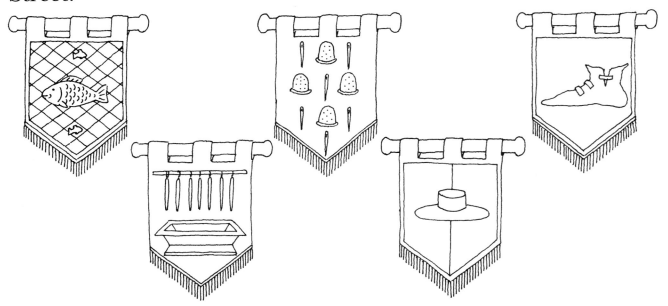

There were guilds of carpenters, tailors, glass makers, painters, weavers, and shoemakers. In fact, almost every kind of work had its own guild. People were not allowed to work in a trade unless they were members of the guild. The important guilds had their own halls. Each guild had a banner that showed the tools of the craft. Can you identify the guilds that owned the banners shown here?

People in the Middle Ages were often known by their first name plus the name of the trade they practised. For example, John the butcher, John the blacksmith, and John the fisherman all lived in the same town. In time these names were shortened to John Butcher, John Smith, and John Fisher. Many people today have last names that began in the Middle Ages.

People who worked in the same trade belonged to a craft club or **guild**. The guilds did a great deal for their members. For example, they fixed the price of goods so that members made a fair profit. No one was allowed to sell too cheaply to take trade away from other members. Also, if a guild member had the tools of his trade stolen, the guild would help him buy replacements. If a husband died

poor, the guild would care for his wife and children. The guild would help a member pay his bills if he was sick and could not work.

The guilds had very strict rules about buying and selling goods. There were rules about the price and quality of articles made by their members. If a baker sold an underweight loaf of bread, he would be fined. He might also be dragged through the streets of the town with the loaf tied around his neck! All the townspeople would laugh and make fun of him.

Another task of the guild was to test all the young apprentices. If a boy wanted to be a craftsman, for example, a baker or a carpenter, he became an apprentice when he was seven years old. His parents paid the master craftsman and the boy went to live with him. For at least seven years, the master taught his apprentice every aspect of the trade. The apprentice received food and clothing at the home of the master. However, he did not get any pay for his work. At the end of this time, each apprentice had to pass an examination before a group of masters. He also had to show an example of his work as proof of his skill. If he passed this test, he became a **journeyman**.

A journeyman was a skilled worker who was paid daily wages. Sometimes he stayed on with his old master, but more often he went off to work for another. A journeyman was still learning the trade. After several years, the journeyman made an example of his best work or a **masterpiece** for the members of the guild to see. If they were pleased, he became a master himself.

From Apprentice to Master

1. A boy becomes an apprentice

2. He learns a trade.

3. He becomes a journeyman.

4. He makes a masterpiece.

SOMETHING TO DO

1. Look at the banners of the guilds. Decide what the design signifies. Design your own banners for these guilds—winemaker, butcher, tailor, goldsmith, locksmith, and painter.

2. Make a list of people you know whose surnames are the same as trades or crafts.

3. Find out what trades still have apprentices today.

People in the Middle Ages did not live as long as people do today. Many children died before they were five years old. The average life expectancy was about thirty years. Why do you think people died so young during the Middle Ages? Let's explore some reasons.

Only rich people could afford to visit a doctor. Doctors thought diseases were caused by different fluids in the body called **humours***. Surgeons operated on patients who were fully awake. Sometimes the patients had to be tied down because they could not bear the pain.*

Today we know that to be strong and healthy, it is necessary to eat the right kinds of foods. A long time ago, people did not worry about a proper diet. They just ate whatever food was available. Even wealthy people did not eat wisely. It was impossible to get fresh fruits and vegetables in the winter.

Sometimes there would be a **famine**. This means that there was very little food. Poor seed, unfertilized land, bad weather, and plant disease were the reasons for crop failure. Many people died during famines for lack of food.

Many of the diseases were caused by lack of proper **hygiene**. Look up the word "hygiene" in your dictionary. Think of the ways you can practice the "principles of keeping well."

Hygiene is as simple as bathing, eating properly prepared food, or drinking clean water. There were no refrigerators in the Middle Ages, so food spoiled easily. If people ate spoiled food, they often got sick. Also, their water supply was not very clean. Open wells meant that all kinds of germs could get into the water. When people drank polluted water, they got sick.

One type of skin disease was **leprosy**. People with this disease were called "lepers." People tried to avoid the lepers because the disease could spread quickly.

Lepers were required to ring a bell as they walked through the streets, so that no one would accidentally come near them.

The worst disease to strike Europe was called the **plague** or the **Black Death**. It was brought from the Far East in the mid-fourteenth century on ships carrying black rats. The disease was first spread by the fleas on the rats when the fleas bit people. Later it spread when a person with the plague breathed on another person. It was probably called the Black Death because the swellings that appeared on sick bodies were black and dark blue.

People tried all kinds of ways to avoid the Black Death. Some carried strong-smelling flowers and herbs. Many city dwellers moved to the country hoping to escape. This only spread the disease to the countryside. Whole villages caught the plague and died. Doctors did not know what to do.

About one-third of the population of Europe may have died from the plague in the fourteenth century. So many people died of the plague that it changed the feudal system forever. After the plague was over there were no longer enough serfs to do all the work.

Every lord wanted his property to be cared for. To get workers for his land, a lord had

Sickness and Treatments

The dirty city conditions helped the plague to spread.

to pay the serfs more than what other lords were paying. Now that the serfs received money instead of goods for their labour, they were much freer. They could move around to work for any lord who offered them the most money. They could buy their own land and were no longer as dependent on the lords for their survival.

After the plague struck Europe, pictures showing the Dance of Death became popular. In these pictures, grinning skeletons led away kings and queens, monks and knights, and merchants and serfs. This showed that death came to everyone, no matter how rich and powerful they were.

SOMETHING TO DO

1. In the 1870s, there was a smallpox epidemic in Canada. Many Aboriginal peoples and settlers died. How are diseases like smallpox controlled today?
2. Talk to your parents and grandparents. Find out if anyone in your family has a home remedy for a cut, burn, or a certain illness. Share the remedy with the class.
3. What is the life expectancy in Canada today? Compare this to life expectancy in the Middle Ages. Why do you think it is higher today?

ir Richard had gone to the marketplace to buy a suit of armour. While he was in the armour-maker's shop, his horse was stolen! Sir Richard believed the thief was Sir Edward, a rival knight, who had wanted Richard's horse. However, Sir Edward denied that he had taken the horse, and the horse was not in Sir Edward's stables.

To prove that he was right, Sir Richard challenged Sir Edward to an **ordeal by battle**. This meant that the two knights would fight to prove who was right.

Sir Edward agreed to the battle. He believed he would win because he had not taken the horse. Sir Edward believed that God would not let harm come to an innocent person.

The next morning, everyone gathered to watch the fight. Each knight had a shield and a weapon similar to a pick-axe. Sir Richard, who was stronger than Sir Edward, soon began to win the battle. When Sir Edward was pinned to the ground with the point of the pick-axe at his throat, he cried "Craven." This meant that he was giving up and accepting defeat. Everyone now believed that Sir Edward was guilty and must be punished.

Do you believe that Sir Edward was guilty or not? What did the ordeal by battle prove?

Many other ways of deciding guilt in the Middle Ages had the same uncertain results as ordeal by battle.

Consider the case of Henry, a homeless wanderer or tramp. He had been accused of murder. Everyone was suspicious of Henry because he was a stranger in town. It was decided to use **ordeal by water** to find out if Henry was guilty.

Henry was taken to the local pond. His hands and feet were tied together and he was thrown into the water.

If Henry sank, it meant that he was innocent. Then he would

Villagers would taunt and throw things at people locked in the stocks.

be rescued. If Henry floated, it was a sign that he was guilty. Then he would be hanged.

After a few moments, Henry began to sink to the bottom. What is the problem with this as a method to decide guilt or innocence?

Meg was a serf. She had been accused of stealing a loaf of bread from the manor's kitchen. The lord of the manor called the village priest to the manor to arrange an **ordeal by fire**. They believed this would show whether Meg had committed the crime.

The priest heated an iron ball in the fire and used tongs to place it in Meg's hand. Meg ran forward three steps and dropped the scalding hot metal. Then the priest bandaged her hand with cloth. He told her that in three days the bandage would be removed. If she had a blister half as large as a walnut, it meant she was guilty.

When the priest removed the bandage on the third day, Meg's hand was covered with a large blister. Without a doubt, she was guilty and must accept her punishment. The usual punishment was to cut off the thief's hand.

As you can see, all these ordeals had one very big problem. No one tried to find out the facts.

About the year 1166, King Henry II of England decided to change things. He declared that twelve men of the town were to be chosen to search out all the facts of a crime. They talked to any witnesses and collected all the information. Then the twelve men made their decision. This was the beginning of the justice system called **trial by jury** that we use today. It was much more fair than any of the ordeals.

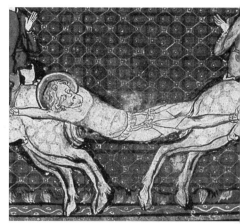

Punishments in the Middle Ages were often severe. They could include being pulled apart between two horses.

SOMETHING TO DO

1. Role play a trial by jury. Use the case of Sir Richard vs. Sir Edward. Pick twelve people to be jurors and one person to be the judge. The rest of the class can be possible witnesses from the village. The jurors should interview witnesses and look for any clues. Act out the trial by jury. Would the outcome of this case be different if there had been trial by jury?

2. Imagine you are living in the Middle Ages. Write an eyewitness account of an ordeal by water or an ordeal by fire that you have watched in your village.

ow did people travel in the Middle Ages? Some main roads were made by the Romans a thousand years before. Many are still usable today. But most other roads were only rough tracks pitted with deep holes. In summer the roads were dry, dusty, and covered with cracks. In winter many roads were impassable. Travellers were often ankle deep in thick mud or snow.

The fastest and easiest way to travel was on horseback. Merchants usually carried their goods by packhorse rather than by horse and carts. Carts were uncomfortable, slow, and very often got stuck. Only kings, queens, and important barons could afford carriages. Wealthy ladies or people who were sick travelled in litters carried between two people. However, most people simply walked wherever they wanted to go.

There were very few inns at that time. Instead, travellers could always stay overnight in the guest room of a monastery. Although the monks did not charge for what they provided, they did expect an offering. Those who could afford it put money in the collection box. A poor person could offer to do a little work to pay for a meal or the room.

Most towns shut their gates at nightfall, and opened them in the morning when it was light. Travellers had much to fear if they continued their journeys in the dark. The woods and forests were hiding places for outlaws and robbers. Even during broad daylight, travellers were held up and robbed in the woods.

It was especially dangerous to travel alone. The countryside was covered by thick forests. These were places where bandits could hide. A lone traveller could be ambushed and never heard from again. For this reason, it was safer for people to travel together in large groups.

Merchants travelling to other countries needed ships to carry their goods. The typical ship at that time had a large square sail and a single mast. Ships could only set out if the wind was blowing in the direction that the captain wanted to go.

Ships did not venture far out into the oceans. Mostly their routes were close to the land. Captains could buy charts showing the features of the coastlines they were going to sail along.

Travelling by Land and Sea

There were many dangers at sea, such as storms, pirates, and enemy ships. For this reason, ships were armed. Soldiers had wooden castles **fore** (front) and **aft** (rear) on the ships to give them protection. From these heights, archers could fire arrows down on the decks of enemy ships. The picture shows a merchant ship built around 1300.

DID YOU KNOW?

Early medieval ships had oars to help them move when there was no wind. They used a steering board or oar on the right side. They called it the "steerboard." This word was shortened to "starboard." Starboard is the word we still use to-day to name the right-hand side of a ship.

SOMETHING TO DO

1. Pretend you are going on a six-week journey. You will be travelling from Venice to Paris. If your horse can travel 54 km in one day, how long will it take to reach Paris? Hint: use your atlas first to determine the distance between Venice and Paris.

2. Compare the merchant ship built in 1300 with the ships that were used to bring the Normans to England in 1066 (shown on page 4). Are there any similarities? What are the differences?

3. It is said that most people in the Middle Ages never travelled more than a couple of kilometres from where they were born. Suggest reasons why this was so.

4. In England, people loved to hear stories about Robin Hood, a robber who lived in the woods and robbed travellers. Locate and read some stories of Robin Hood and his Merry Men. Describe the character Robin Hood portrays. Can you identify the forces of good and evil? How do you feel about Robin Hood's actions? Do you think there really was a Robin Hood? Write a Robin Hood tale of your own.

 n the Middle Ages there were advanced civilizations in Asia that the people of Europe knew very little about. However, Nicolo and Maffeo Polo had heard of the riches of China. At that time China was known as Cathay. The Polo brothers were merchants in the Italian city of Venice. In 1271, they set sail for Cathay taking with them Nicolo's seventeen-year-old son, Marco.

The Polos sailed east on the Mediterranean Sea. Then they travelled by land, sometimes on horses, sometimes on camels, and sometimes on foot. Their journey took three years. Finally, they arrived in the palace of the Kublai Khan, the ruler of Cathay.

The Polos stayed for seventeen years in Cathay. Marco Polo studied the languages of China. He became a favourite of the Kublai Khan. The Khan sent Marco on fact-finding trips to many different parts of his empire. Marco Polo visited places in Asia where no other European had ever been.

In 1292 the Polos said farewell to the Khan and returned home. When they arrived in Venice, at first their friends and relatives did not believe the Polos' tales of adventure.

News of Marco's adventures spread throughout Europe. He published a book called *Description of the World.* In it he described the kingdoms he had visited and the customs of the people he had met. Marco told stories of the Kublai Khan, the wonders of his court, and the beautiful cities of China. Marco told of places where he had seen fishermen dive for handfuls of valuable pearls. He spoke of islands full of wonderful spices and palaces that were roofed with gold.

Marco Polo's book gave the people of Europe some of their first ideas about the East. It showed that there was a great civilization in China, in some ways better than the one in Europe. It told of riches far beyond anything Europeans could imagine. Later, a young sea captain, named Christopher Columbus, read the book about Marco's travels and decided to seek a sea route to Cathay.

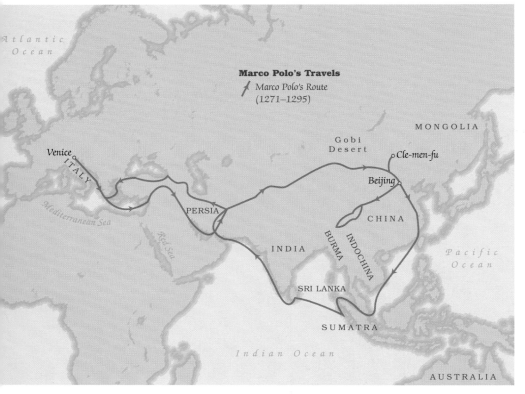

Marco Polo's Travels

Marco Polo's Route (1271–1295)

The Adventures of Marco Polo

Marco Polo saw many strange animals on his journey that were unfamiliar to Europeans. This is how he described one of these.

There were huge serpents, ten metres long and over a metre wide across their body. At the front, near their head, they have two short legs which have three claws like those of a tiger. Their eyes are larger than a cream bun, and very bright. Their jaws are wide enough to swallow a man. They have huge sharp teeth. They look so fierce that neither men nor any kind of animal can go near them without being terrified. . . . In the daytime to avoid great heat, they hide in caves. From there at night, they travel to find their food. They eat any animal they can grab—whether tiger, wolf, or any other. After this, they drag themselves toward some lake, spring, or river in order to drink. Because of their great weight as they move along the shore, they make a deep mark, as if a heavy log had been dragged along the sands.

To prove their stories were true, the Polos gave a feast. Afterwards, Marco brought out the clothes they had been wearing when they returned to Venice. He ripped open the seams of the garments. Out dropped diamonds, rubies, emeralds, and other precious gems. At the sight of so much wealth, everyone was convinced of the Polos' tales.

SOMETHING TO DO

1. What animal do you think Marco Polo was describing? What parts of his description sound as though they might be exaggerated, or even untrue?

2. Write your own account about an animal you have seen or describe something your pet does that is unusual.

3. Make a list of the seas, oceans, and countries that Marco Polo travelled through. Use an atlas to find out what modern countries are now located in the area known earlier as Persia.

slam is a religion whose followers worship one God named Allah. This religion was started by Mohammed, who was born in the holy city of Mecca. In 610 Mohammed became the prophet of Allah. One day, when Mohammed was in the desert, an angel came to him. The angel told Mohammed Allah's commandments. From time to time over the next twenty years the angel came with more words from Allah.

A young Muslim reading from the Koran.

All the sayings the angel told Mohammed were written down in a book. It became the holy book of Islam. It was called the Qur'an (Koran). The Qur'an was written in Arabic. It told Muslims, the followers of Mohammed, the basic beliefs of Islam and how they should live. According to the Qur'an, Muslims should not eat pork, drink liquor, or gamble. The Qur'an also gave advice on marriage, divorce, and business practices.

The Qur'an sets out the **five pillars of Islam**. These are the most important duties of all who believe in Allah.

1. Everyone must believe there is one God and that Mohammed is his prophet.
2. Everyone must turn to face Mecca and kneel on a prayer mat to pray at least five times a day.
3. Everyone must give to the poor.
4. For one month each year Muslims must **fast**. This means they cannot eat, drink, or smoke from sunrise until sunset. They call this holy month **Ramadan**.
5. Everyone who can do so must try to visit Mecca once in a lifetime.

The centre of worship of Islam was not a church or synagogue, but a **mosque**. Mosques were

The Blue Mosque in Istanbul.

beautiful inside as well as out. The floors were covered by prayer mats which worshippers knelt on to pray. Lamps of fine glass hung from the ceilings. In some mosques there were windows of coloured glass but there were no pictures or statues of people or living creatures. Islam taught that only Allah could create life. It was sinful to try to act like Allah by drawing

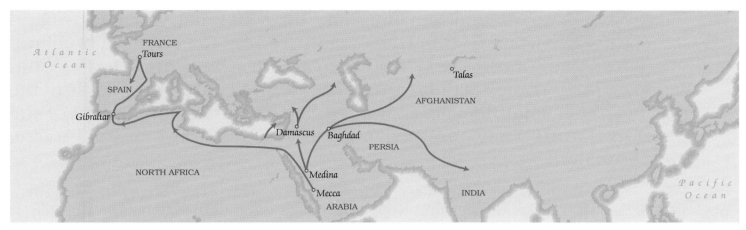

living creatures. Instead, on the walls and ceilings, Muslim artists made designs or patterns of lines.

Outside the mosque was a tower called a **minaret**. Five times a day a man climbed the tower. He called to the people that it was time to pray. Whatever Muslims were doing, they stopped to pray. Prayers in the mosque were led by an **imam** or prayer leader.

Islam spread rapidly. Mohammed's wish was to carry his religion to other people. This was done by fighting "holy wars" against "enemies of Allah" or nations where the people did not believe in Islam. The armies of Islam quickly conquered their neighbours. By 750, all the lands from Spain through North Africa to the north of India had become Muslim.

Islamic countries were very civilized. The people were advanced in medicine. Muslim doctors used surgery to fight diseases. They knew that disease was not the work of devils. They knew it had natural causes. The Arabs also learned about **astronomy**, the study of the stars and planets. They built buildings and instruments for looking at the stars. They loved poetry and stories. A famous collection of their stories is called *The Arabian Nights*. They loved music and beautiful gardens with flowers, pools of water, and trees. The Arabs invented our modern numbers. They made better maps and found new ways of steering ships at sea. They invented instruments like the **astrolabe**, which helped sailors find their way at sea. The better maps and the astrolabe helped them when they went on long journeys to trade with other countries.

The Spread of Islam to 750.

SOMETHING TO DO

1. Draw five pillars across one page of your notebook. Label the drawing The Five Pillars of Islam. On each pillar write in one of the five duties of Islam.

2. Locate a copy of *The Arabian Nights* in your school or public library. Read some of the stories. Select one story, such as The Story of Queen Scheherezade, and act it out for the class.

erusalem is a holy city for Muslims, Christians, and Jews. In 638 it was captured by the soldiers of Islam. For the next 400 years Christians and Jews could travel safely to Jerusalem. Then, in 1071 fierce Islamic soldiers called Seljuk Turks got control of the Holy Land. They stopped Christians and Jews from visiting Jerusalem.

When news of events in the Holy Land reached Europe, Christians were very angry. The Pope, head of the Christian church, spoke to a large crowd. He said that instead of fighting each other, Christians should all go to war against the Turks. He told them of rich fertile regions in the Holy Land where knights could live in comfort. He promised that God would pardon the sins of those who went to fight the Turks. He encouraged soldiers to go to Jerusalem to drive out the Turks. These wars were called **Crusades**, the wars of the cross. The knights who went on the Crusades were called **Crusaders**. They wore a red cross as a badge on their tunics. Knights and soldiers left England, Germany, and France to fight in the Holy Land. Some went because they thought that was what God wanted. Others were looking for money, land, or adventure.

In 1099 the Crusaders reached Jerusalem and captured the holy city. They looted the city, taking gold, silver, horses, and all kinds of goods found in the houses. For the next 71 years Jerusalem was controlled by the Christians.

In 1170 Islam found a new leader. He was a brilliant general named Saladin. In 1187 Saladin's army recaptured Jerusalem. In 1199 another Crusade set out from Europe to try to capture it back again. This time the Crusade was lead by King Richard the Lionheart of England. Although he won many battles against the Muslims, Richard failed to capture Jerusalem. Several other Crusades were fought during the thirteenth century.

King Richard the Lionheart leads a Crusader army into the Holy Land.

The saddest of all Crusades was the Children's Crusade. About 30 000 French children were led by a peasant boy named Stephen. They set sail from France in 1212. Most of the children never reached the Holy Land. Along the way they were captured by Christian merchants and sold into slavery!

The Europeans did not win any of them.

In 1291 the Muslims captured the city of Acre, the last Christian stronghold in the Holy Land. The Muslims had won the Crusades. They now ruled all of the territory that the Crusaders had fought to control.

The Crusades brought Europeans into closer contact with the Muslim lands in the East. From the Muslims they learned many new ideas and took them back to Europe. They brought home carpets, tapestries, and richly woven cloth to put in their castles. They learned new glass-making techniques, and they discovered how to keep silkworms so they could make silk garments. They also began to use spices, such as pepper, with their food and to grow new crops, such as sugarcane and plums. Slowly there grew up a trade link between Europe and the East. Europe was no longer cut off from the rest of the world.

The brilliant Islamic general, Saladin. Richard the Lionheart and Saladin were arch-enemies. One day when their armies were fighting, Saladin heard that Richard's horse had been killed. Saladin immediately stopped fighting and ordered that two horses from his own stable be sent to Richard. Do you think the Muslim soldiers also followed a Code of Chivalry?

SOMETHING TO DO

1. Why did the Crusaders wear a red cross on their tunics?

2. Make a timeline of the Crusades. Draw a line from the top of a page of blank paper to the bottom, about 4 cm from the left-hand side. Label the left-hand column "Date" and the right hand column "Event." Unscramble all of the dates below and put them in the correct chronological order. Beside each date write a brief description in the event column of what happened during that year. The dates for your timeline are: 1291, 638, 1170, 1071, 1187, 1199, 1099, 1212.

3. What happened during the Children's Crusade?

4. If you had heard the Pope speak, would you have gone on a Crusade? Explain.

tories of the adventures of the Crusaders and Marco Polo spread through Europe. The people of Europe wanted to wear silks from Cathay and perfumes and jewels from India. They wished to taste the new foods and spices from Asia. They wanted luxury items such as carpets and wall hangings to decorate their dwellings. Soon a bustling trade developed between Europe and the East.

Overland journeys from the East were long, hard, and dangerous. Merchants travelled together in caravans for safety. Trains of slow moving camels were laden with goods. Merchants from Asia brought their goods as far as the ports of the eastern Mediterranean Sea. There the camels were unloaded. Then the goods were put on ships and brought to Venice or Genoa by merchants from Europe. From Venice and Genoa the goods were carried by different trade routes to places all over Europe. The journey from China to Europe and back often took three years.

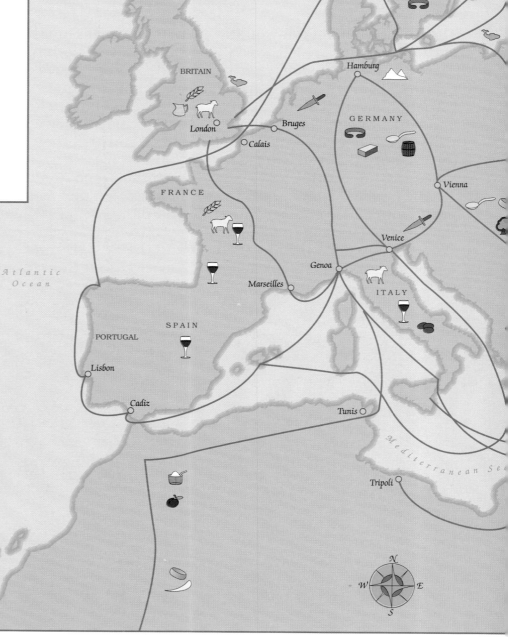

Trade With the East

SOMETHING TO DO

Look at the picture on pp. 60-61 of some of the products brought by traders and Crusaders from the East.

1. Make a list of them in your notebook.

2. Pretend you are a merchant from the East who wishes to sell these goods to Europeans. Choose one item and create an advertisement for it. Include such things as what it looks like; how it is used; and where it comes from. Don't forget to tell them how it will improve their lives. Remember your customers may never have seen these goods before. Illustrate your advertisement with pictures. Draw them yourself or cut them out of your own magazines from home.

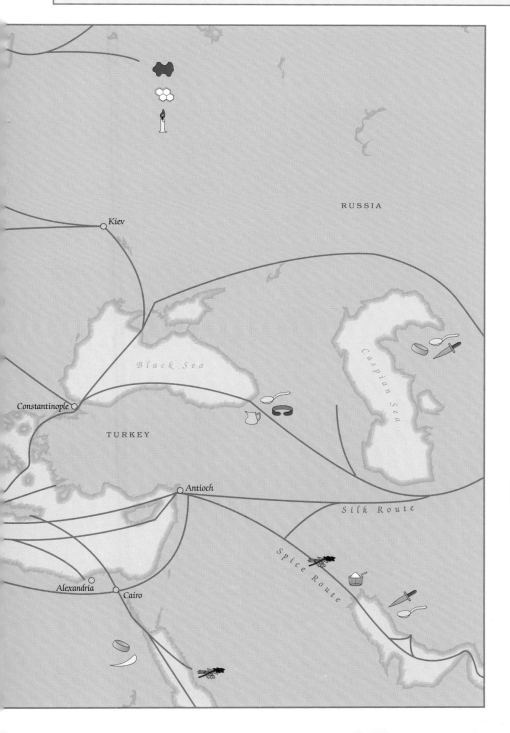

FINDING INFORMATION FROM A MAP

Look at the map of trade routes.

1. Suppose you are bringing silk from China to Britain. Point out the land route you would use to reach the Mediterranean Sea. Point out the sea route you would use to get the silk to Italy. By what route would the silk go from Italy to Britain?

2. What goods could a merchant from Britain offer in exchange for spices from the East?

3. Why did Venice become an important trading centre?

4. What products do England and France have to trade that are the same?

5. Where is the closest place that France could get olives? What could France offer that country that it might need?

By the early 1200s, trade routes connected Europe with parts of Africa and the East.

59

JEWELLERY

PERFUME

ROCK CRYSTAL

MIRROR

ASTROLABE

BRASS

NUTMEG

PORCELAIN

GINGER

RICE

ALMONDS

B

ARABIC NUMERALS

Trade With the East

WALL HANGINGS

SATINS, SILKS, VELVETS, AND DYES

CLOTH EMBROIDERED WITH GOLD

DATES

RAISINS

GREEN FIGS

PER

FORKS

CARPETS

n the Middle Ages fashions changed more slowly than they do today. However, fashions certainly did change. Meet some typical people of the Middle Ages. Look at the drawings to see what fashions were like and how they changed over the course of time.

EARLY MIDDLE AGES—AROUND THE YEAR 1100

Lady Matilde is dressed for a feast in the castle's Great Hall. She wears a blue woollen gown that fits close to her body. It has embroidered sleeves that almost touch the floor. Her jewelled belt is wrapped twice around the waist and knotted in front. Her red cloak is fastened across the shoulders with a cord. Her head is covered with a single piece of white linen held in place with a circle of metal. Beside Lady Matilde is her husband, Baron Hugh. There is surprisingly little difference between the clothes worn by men and by women. Hugh wears a grey wool undertunic with tight sleeves. Over this, the baron wears a sleeveless outer brown tunic. It is fastened around the waist by a chained belt. When it is chilly, Baron Hugh wears a long blue coat which he fastens over his shoulder with a brooch. Important people wore long cloaks; poor people like serfs wore them to the knee. The hem of the cloak is decorated with a colourful band of embroidery. Hugh's legs are covered with thick stockings made of cloth. He wears shoes of soft leather that are buckled or strapped over the tops of his feet.

Serfs trudging to work in Baron Hugh's fields wear peasant clothes. Tom wears a rough, homespun tunic. The fabric must keep him warm when it is cold outside. In winter Tom covers the tunic with a cloak. The cloak is not lined with fur, but with sheepskin. He also wraps long strips of cloth around

Baron Hugh and Lady Matilde

Elizabeth and Tom

his legs to keep him warm. Tom cannot afford leather shoes. If it is really muddy, he works barefoot in the fields. In winter, Tom wears heavy, clumsy wooden shoes called **clogs**.

Elizabeth also wears a tunic made out of the same rough material. It is heavy and shapeless. When Elizabeth works in the fields alongside Tom, she tucks the skirt inside her belt. Both Elizabeth and Tom wear hoods. In stormy weather, the hood is pulled up over the head to keep the neck, ears, and head warm.

LATE MIDDLE AGES —AROUND THE YEAR 1400

Lady Sarah is the wife of a prosperous wool merchant. She lived three hundred years after Lady Matilde.

Lady Sarah is wearing a deep blue cloak lined with cream-coloured satin. Under the dress she wears an undergarment of white silk. From her waist hang the keys to the rooms and cupboards of the manor house. Notice that women's hats have become very elaborate. Lady Sarah's is made of deep blue fabric. The hat is decorated with embroidery and beautiful jewels.

William Grevell, Lady Sarah's husband, earned his wealth from the wool business. William's hair is very thick on the top of his head. However, it is cut high above his ears, leaving the part below shaved and bare. This was a very popular style of the 1400s.

William wears a very full garment called a surcoat. It ends just above his knees. The surcoat is made of crimson velvet trimmed with fox fur.

William's stockings are in two colours. One is red, while the other is white. By 1400 men's shoes had become long and pointed. Sometimes shoes were so long the tips of the shoes had to be fastened to the knees with jewelled chains.

In Lady Sarah's time the serfs' clothes are still the same. Poor people's clothes did not change very much. It was actually a crime for peasants to wear nice clothes. A law said that "no ploughman, oxherd, cowherd, shepherd, swineherd, dairywoman, or anyone else who works as a farmer should wear anything but cheap cloth or blanket."

William Grevell and Lady Sarah

SOMETHING TO DO

1. Find out more about costumes by looking at historical fashion books in libraries. Create a mural to show fashions in the Middle Ages. Use drawings and brief descriptions to show samples of the costumes of this period.

2. "There is surprisingly little difference between clothes worn by men and women in the Middle Ages." What evidence can you find to prove this statement from the pictures in this book?

lossary

abbot the head monk of a monastery.

abbot's guest house a house for travellers staying at a monastery.

abbot's house the large house where the abbot lived and entertained guests.

aft the back of a ship

alms gifts of money for the poor.

alms house the place in an abbey where poor people can stay and receive gifts of food or money.

Angles the old word for the English people.

apprentice a young person who learns a trade from a master.

armour protective covering of any kind.

arrow storm a large number of arrows fired at the enemy all at the same time.

astrolabe an instrument that helped sailors chart their course at sea.

astronomy the study of the stars and planets.

bailey an open space enclosed by the outer wall of a castle.

bailiff the overseer on a manor.

bargain to argue over the price of something.

baron a person who was given land by the king or queen and promised service in return.

battering ram a machine used to break through the gate of a castle.

Battle of Hastings battle in 1066 in which William the Conqueror defeated and killed King Harold of England.

Bayeux Tapestry a piece of linen more than 70 metres long that contains embroidered pictures of the Battle of Hastings.

blood-letting removing some of a person's blood to cure them of disease.

canopied beds beds with tops over them, surrounded by thick curtains on all sides to keep out cold air.

chain mail armour suits worn by soldiers made of thousands of tiny metal rings fastened together.

charity help freely given to needy people.

chastity the state of not being married.

church the place of worship in Christian religions.

cistern a stone tank for collecting rainwater.

clogs heavy wooden shoes.

cloister a covered walkway with a wall on one side and columns on the other.

concentric a pattern with one circle inside another.

crusader a knight who went on the Crusades.

Crusades the series of wars fought between Christians and Muslims over possession of the Holy Land.

dormitory the sleeping quarters in a monastery.

dowry the amount of money that a bride brought into a marriage.

dubbing the ceremony in which a squire becomes a knight.

evidence clues or facts that show what happened at a certain time and place.

famine extreme scarcity of food in an area.

fast to go without any food for a certain period of time.

flail a long stick used to beat out kernels of grain.

flaming catapult a machine used to throw balls of fire into a castle under siege.

fore the front part of a ship.

gatehouse the fortified part of a castle that protects the gate.

great hall the part of a castle where the lord and lady eat their meals and entertain their guests.

guild an association for the common good of people who practice a certain trade.

habit the uniform of a nun or monk.

hawking same as falconry. Hunting with birds of prey.

high table a raised table where the lord and lady of a castle ate with their honored guests.

humours a medieval medical term for different fluids in the body.

hygiene the science of staying in good health.

imam a Muslim prayer leader.

infirmary a small hospital.

inner curtain a thick wall protecting the inner ward of a castle.

inner ward an open area in the middle of a castle.

jetty the upper story of a house that hung over the street.

journeyman a skilled worker who is paid daily wages.

joust a contest in which two knights on horseback try to knock each other to the ground.

keep the stronghold of a castle, where the lord and lady lived.

knight a trained soldier who promised loyalty and service to a baron.

leprosy a very serious skin disease.

lists the fenced-in area where the jousts of a tournament are held.

mangon a machine for hurling heavy rocks at a castle wall.

manor a piece of land that a king gives a vassal in return for loyalty and service.

master a skilled craftsperson who teaches a trade to an apprentice.